MATT & HEID
WITH RACHEL MCMURRAY-BRANSCOMBE

A CHRISTMAS
DEVOTIONAL

First edition October 2018

Scripture quotations are taken from the Holy Bible, New Living Translation, copyright ©1996, 2004, 2015 by Tyndale House Foundation. Used by permission of Tyndale House Publishers, Inc., Carol Stream, Illinois 60188. All rights reserved.

Book design by Curt McMurray-Branscombe
Illustrations and cover copyright © 2018
www.fountainst.com

ISBN 978-0-692-04399-8 (hardback)
ISBN 978-0-692-04402-5 (ebook)

www.mattmessner.com

Table of Contents

How to Use This Book

Welcome to *Advent Encounter*. It's our prayer that this devotional will guide you and your loved ones throughout the Christmas season, providing moments of reflection, celebration and discussion. In our own family, we have a rich history of participating in Advent. Along with our two children, we would usually assemble a simple Advent wreath with candles. Then, on each Sunday night leading up to Christmas Eve, we would sit as a family on the couch, read the Bible, light the candle, discuss the reading and pray. Often, we would sing a Christmas carol as well. It helped us all focus on the real reason for the season.

We know this can be a busy season, and adding one more item to your "to-do" list can seem like a burden, but we encourage you to find rest here. Use this devotional to take a break, unplug from all the chaos and experience your own Advent Encounter.

HISTORY OF ADVENT

Although the exact beginning of Advent is hard to determine, it is often attributed to fourth-century Europe. It was originally designed as a time of preparation for new converts getting ready to be baptized on Epiphany (a celebration of when the Magi visited Jesus). This was later expanded to include a time of preparation for the entire Christmas season.

For the early Christians, Advent was not only focused on the *first* coming of Christ (Christmas), but also looked forward to the Second Coming, when Christ will return. For that reason, Advent was divided into two periods: the first two weeks were focused on the Second Coming, observed through fasting and confession of sins; the last two weeks focused on Christmas, observed through celebration. In this way, Christians never separated the two comings of Christ—they are forever linked.

WHAT YOU'LL NEED

You're welcome to participate in Advent as traditionally or as creatively as you desire. Keep it the same every year, or mix it up, it's your call! People discover countless ways to display their candles—from wreaths, to Advent logs, to decorative vases. (In our home, there were some "busy" years where we simply arranged five tea light candles in a circle.) For your candles, stick to the classic colors or find colors that match your values for the season.

Traditionally, participation in Advent would include a wreath with four or five candles. Three candles are purple (for the first three weeks), one candle is pink (for the fourth week) and the last candle is white (for Christmas Eve/Day).

If you're interested, here is a little of the symbolism that goes into the traditional set-up:

> The circular **wreath** symbolizes how Christ is eternal and without end.
>
> The **purple candles** symbolize prayer, penance and preparation.
>
> The **pink candle** symbolizes rejoicing.
>
> And the **white candle** symbolizes the birth of Jesus.

But we invite you to find the expression of Advent that works best for you. It's the *spirit of Advent* and not the *rules of Advent* that we're encouraging in this devotional.

In addition to five candles, you'll need access to the Internet to watch the weekly videos.

WHO CAN DO THIS STUDY TOGETHER

Our hope is that this devotional will meet you right where you are. We invite you to participate as a family, as a small group or in a personal time of reflection. There's no right or wrong group for this devotional—wherever you are, whomever you're with, encounter Advent together!

WEEKLY BREAKDOWN

Advent traditionally begins four Sundays before Christmas. So pull out your calendar, find Christmas day, then count back four Sundays—that's going to be the first week of this devotional. Each of the first four chapters will coincide with a Sunday. You can complete the last chapter on Christmas Eve or Christmas Day, whichever you prefer.

Within each week, we've developed various elements designed to focus on the theme of that week. Here is the rundown of each chapter:

Devotional Reading

Each week begins with a story. This story can be enjoyed together around the Advent table or read individually throughout the week (depending on the reading levels and time available to the group). While these stories are "family-friendly," we encourage you to determine which elements will best suit your family's needs.

A quick reminder: though some story details may be borrowed from past sermons or our personal journeys, these stories are complete works of fiction. No people or events are based on anything in real life. The purpose of these fictional stories is to illustrate the theme of the week.

Online Videos

Online videos are an important element for this process. It allows us to get a better look at the values of the week and often helps connect the stories to the Advent activities. It also provides a way for us to speak directly to you, sharing our personal thoughts and blessings for the week. So pull up a phone, laptop, tablet or TV and enjoy these Advent videos.

These videos come *free* with your purchase of this devotional. You can access the videos here:

www.mattmessner.com/advent

Scripture Reading

As a spiritual practice, take turns reading the selected Bible passage aloud. Let this element inform the message of the week—it's the foundation of our celebration!

Candle Lighting

Each week, you'll light one more candle than the previous week. For the first Sunday, you'll light one candle. On the second Sunday, you'll light the previous week's candle, as well as a new one. And so on. While doing this, someone can volunteer to read aloud the included text.

We would also like to encourage fire safety. Please make sure you are lighting candles in appropriate ways. This includes determining *who* gets to light the candle and *where* the candle is located in your home. Always remember to extinguish your candles at the end of your Advent activities.

Prayer

You can reflect on the prayers aloud as a group or individually. Take turns reading it around the table, or each person can agree while reading the prayer silently. Whatever you decide, God will hear you!

Discussion Questions

Finally, we've included discussion questions, reflecting on all the content from that week. While we'd love for you to use these questions to prompt life-giving conversations around the dinner table or within a small group setting, we also think there is great value in journaling

9

responses to these questions. In whatever way you decide to respond, please take some time for group- or self-reflection. The purpose of this element is to consider our response to the week's readings and activities, making sure we translate them into action in our daily lives.

Many blessings as you begin your Advent encounter and merry Christmas!

Advent Week
— 1 —
ENCOUNTER HOPE

Christmas is the story of hope—hope fulfilled and hope instilled. The coming of Jesus was the answer to a plea, the realization of a promise, the embodiment of a prophecy.

But hope doesn't end at Christmas; it begins there. Hope for the future, for families and friends. Hope is found in what has already happened, and what has yet to happen.

In the flurry of Christmas magic, it's easy to confuse hope with a wish, something we would add to a holiday list of "wants." But hope isn't a hesitant wish that God would be, or could be, faithful and true. It's the confident expectation that He cannot be anything but faithful and true.

*And faith? Well, that's when we put hope into mo-
tion. It whispers, "Take heart and take action."
And we do.*

*All because of promises and prophecies. All because of
hope.*

All because of Christmas.

S urrounded by moving boxes, Kim sighed. She couldn't find her favorite baking dish. It was the latest missing family heirloom, probably buried deep in the corners of their new rental home. Hopefully,
it wasn't broken, but after moving four times in six months, who could
say?

It was Thanksgiving morning.

On other Thanksgivings, not *this* Thanksgiving, her house would
be filled with the smells of food, the sounds of children watching the
parade, the joy of a day off school or work.

But today, her house was empty, except for the boxes. Silent, but for
the few muffled grunts from Paul, who was unpacking upstairs.

She stood, stretching from days of tedious packing and unpacking.
As she walked to her fridge, she already knew what she'd find inside:
nothing. In all the chaos of moving (yet again), they'd missed their
chance to pick up food for the holiday. They'd polished off the leftover
Chinese food late the previous night, leaving their kitchen bare.

What were her kids doing right now? Were they preparing their
own dinners? Getting ready for the big football game? Following family traditions?

Through the kitchen window, she could see the leaves changing color, falling to the ground in geometric patterns. The chill in the air reminded Kim that Christmas was coming. As a pastor, she always looked forward to this time of year. It was a season for celebration, for special candlelit services, for filling her house with loved ones. True, she missed the big events she used to host—the dinners and parties. But she ached for the small moments, like when her kids would open a Christmas Eve gift.

"Just one? How about two?" they would plead.

Kim and Paul would laugh and reply, "Just one. You'll have to wait until tomorrow for the rest!"

She always loved how Thanksgiving came before the Christmas season. It was a chance to be grateful for all that she had...but it also made room in her heart for all the things she would look forward to in the coming weeks. Theirs had been a house of joyful anticipation.

Pausing in that silent, empty room, Kim wondered, what did she have to look forward to this year?

Paul bounded down the steps. Feeling energized from his productivity (he'd unpacked two rooms already!), he felt like he should check on Kim. As he turned toward the kitchen, he saw her frame leaning against the window, unmoving. After thirty years of marriage, he could read his wife's body language. She was grieving.

Pausing on the bottom step, Paul was unsure what to do next. What could he possibly say or do to ease a mother's first holiday without her children?

"So," he began, "it's Thanksgiving. What do you think we should today?"

Kim turned to face him. "I'm not sure. We don't have any food in the house, and I can't find any of our kitchenware in all...this." She absently pointed to the stacks of boxes.

"Right," Paul said. "Then I guess we should probably eat out tonight."

"Where? Everything's closed."

"Not everything," Paul said with a smile. He just had a great idea! "Denny's is always open."

Kim gave him a look he knew well—she would need convincing.

"Hear me out," he said. "It could be fun. Or at least, funny. I've always wanted to go to Denny's on a holiday. Besides, then we won't have to do any dishes." He decided not to add: "What other choice do we have?"

But perhaps Kim had already thought of this because she gave him a resigned smile and a small nod. They would be going to Denny's for Thanksgiving.

Driving through their small town, Paul gazed out the window. They had moved to Forest Hill six months ago, leaving behind their church, their family and their lifelong friends. This new community still held that feeling of foreignness.

As they passed the rows of houses, warm lights peeked through curtains, inviting loved ones into the glowing comfort of home. Paul could imagine families sitting down to pray, eat, drink, laugh, tell stories, remember. Was Kim thinking about their old house right now? It had been their dream home, miraculously provided by God. But when that same God called them to Forest Hill in the middle of a recession, they sold it for a loss.

The businesses in town were all closed for the night, as if to say to any passerby: "Go home and be with those you love. This is no time to be out and about."

At the very end of town, however, one sign was still humming with neon light. The rotating Denny's logo acted as a beacon for their truck, drawing them through the dark to the only place they could get a Thanksgiving dinner.

Paul parked, surprised to find several other cars in the lot. Apparently, they weren't the only ones with nowhere to go on this holiday.

Inside, they picked a secluded booth in the back corner, both choosing the "Thanksgiving Special" from the menu (complete with sliced turkey, stuffing and mashed potatoes). In the booths surrounding them, couples sat quietly working on their food. A few single people idled alone, glazed eyes locked on their phone screens. But there were no families, there was no laughter.

Paul turned to look at his wife, for whom cooking was one of life's great pleasures, diligently cutting through the turkey slices. This wasn't as fun, or funny, as he'd hoped it would be. Though she didn't complain, he knew this was a far cry from what they'd envisioned God was promising them. What if it never got better? Is this what all future holidays would look like? Christmas was coming, after all…

Kim's voice interrupted his thoughts. "Advent starts this weekend. Are you ready?"

It was his turn to preach the Sunday sermon and he'd spent the morning in prayer and reflection trying to prepare. He had little to show for it.

Picking at his mashed potatoes, Paul said, "This year may be a little harder than other years."

"Let's see," Kim paused to think, "this weekend is the Prophecy Candle—the symbol of hope."

"Exactly. It hits a little close to home. This wasn't exactly what we had in mind when we pictured a new, fresh season in life."

Kim looked at her husband. "Do you doubt God called us here?"

"Not for a minute." In that, Paul felt confident. "But I'll admit these last six months haven't gone the way we hoped they would."

Kim gave her husband a half-smile and said, "Like, when our house didn't sell, and we had to jump from borrowed guest room to guest room for months, virtually homeless? Or how we haven't been able to visit our kids in months? Or that we're celebrating Thanksgiving in a room full of strangers?"

Paul nodded. "Yeah, like those things." He would need to speak about hope in the coming weekend service, even though his own expectations had been met with disappointment.

Kim sat for a moment before she said, "I guess hope is what we have while we wait."

Paul's heart filled with a little more love for his wife in that moment. "So, you still feel it? Hope?"

"To be honest, I don't always feel it. I don't always see how things will work out, but I choose to believe they will. In the meantime, we can be obedient. If that isn't an expression of hope, what is?"

Paul reached over and took his wife's hand. "So, what do you think our next hope-filled step of obedience should be?"

Kim smiled at her husband, and her smile lit up her face.

This was Kim's favorite part of the Christmas Eve candlelight service. She gazed out at all the lights twinkling in the darkness. The flames hovered and danced, held aloft by hands young and old.

She looked down at her own brightly-lit candle, a reminder that just one glimmer of hope can outshine the doubts of life.

To conclude the service, Paul and Kim, standing side-by-side in the pulpit, offered a final prayer and blessing.

The lights snapped on, drawing everyone back to the present—to their Christmas Eve plans, the guests visiting from out of town, the gifts yet-to-be-wrapped. Parishioners blew out their candles, wished each other a blessed holiday, slipped on their coats, gathered their children and ventured out into the chilly night air.

Kim moved as quickly as the rest, packing up her Bible and purse. She and Paul had plans for that night.

They raced home, their truck winding through the now more-familiar streets of their neighborhood. As they approached their rented house, they could make out several other cars already parked in front of their home. Running inside, they greeted the faces they saw:

There was Kevin, the college student who couldn't afford to go home over Christmas break.

And Charlotte, their elderly neighbor, whose children never came to visit.

Setting the table were Sean and Kevin, a single father and his son.

Tom and Janet were talking near the Christmas tree. Both had moved to Forest Hill in the past few months—one for a factory job, the other for the military.

Becky was pulling something out of the oven (putting Kim's favorite baking dish to good use). A waitress at Denny's, Becky had just got off her Christmas Eve shift and wouldn't have had time to prepare a whole meal for her children, who were playing in the front foyer. Fortunately, now Becky didn't have to.

Looking around, Kim's house was full, and so was her heart. Paul and Kim had decided in that Denny's booth on Thanksgiving to take a step of hope, of faith. They had been called to love the people of Forest Hill, and that's exactly what they would do—with the confident expectation that God would be faithful and that He would use them for good. Each person in their home that Christmas Eve had nowhere else to go. That is, until they were invited to dinner by Paul and Kim.

Kim paused for only a moment before snapping into action. Everyone had pitched in to begin preparing the meal while Paul and Kim finished at the church, but there were still rolls that needed to be put in the oven. On her way to the kitchen, Kim greeted each of her guests with a genuine hug and smile. They were welcome here.

She reached the kitchen, now free of moving boxes, just as a figure stepped out from behind the pantry door. Two figures, in fact.

Kim gasped, tears filling her eyes.

"Merry Christmas, Mom," said her daughter and son in unison.

In one quick motion, Kim wrapped both her children in a deep hug, laughing and crying all at once. She was vaguely aware of everyone else in the room rejoicing and clapping. After holding them for a long while, she stepped back to find a misty-eyed Paul.

"What...? How did this happen? Did you know?" All of Kim's questions poured out at once.

Paul just smiled, hugging his children and his wife.

As everyone sat down to Christmas Eve dinner, hope was alive, shining like a candle dancing in the night.

I heard the bells on Christmas Day
Their old, familiar carols play,
and wild and sweet The words repeat
Of peace on earth, good-will to men!

And in despair I bowed my head;
"There is no peace on earth," I said;
"For hate is strong, And mocks the song
Of peace on earth, good-will to men!"

Then pealed the bells more loud and deep:
"God is not dead, nor doth He sleep;
The Wrong shall fail, The Right prevail,
With peace on earth, good-will to men."

"I Heard the Bells on Christmas Day"
Henry Wadsworth Longfellow

 Please take some time now to watch the video for this week's Advent focus. You can find the video at mattmessner.com/advent.

SCRIPTURE READING

Please have someone read aloud:

Isaiah 9:2

The people who walk in darkness
will see a great light.
For those who live in a land of deep darkness,
a light will shine.

Isaiah 9:6-7

For a child is born to us,
a son is given to us.
The government will rest on his shoulders.
And he will be called:
Wonderful Counselor, Mighty God,
Everlasting Father, Prince of Peace.
His government and its peace
will never end.
He will rule with fairness and justice from the throne
of his ancestor David
for all eternity.
The passionate commitment of the Lord of Heaven's
Armies will make this happen!

CANDLE LIGHTING

While one person lights the candle, please have someone read:

As we light the Prophecy Candle, we think about God's promises. Each promise fills us with hope. The Bible is full of promises.

In the Old Testament, God promised his people a Savior. They waited for Jesus, who would save us and reign forever as King.

In the New Testament, Jesus promised us He would return. Christians all over the world look forward to that day.

Today, we also have promises from God for our lives. He knows the future and we can have hope in Him. God is always good, and God will always keep His promises.

PRAYER

Jesus,

You are Immanuel—God with us. We celebrate that you fulfilled the prophecy, the promise. You came all those years ago, providing us with unending hope.

On this first week of Advent, we set aside time to anticipate the coming of Christmas.

In our lives, may we choose hope.
In our doubts, may we walk in faith.
In our actions, may we obey.
In our waiting, may we remember Your goodness.
And if we lack any of these, may we rely on Your strength.

Thank You for being the constant source of our hope.

In Your name we pray,

Amen.

✶ DISCUSSION QUESTIONS ✶

1. What is one thing you are hoping for in this Christmas season? (Nothing is too big or small!)

2. Do you feel like you've ever lost hope? What happened?

3. Hope is linked with obedience—it's taking a faithful step, trusting that God is always good and faithful. Where do you see this true in your life? What faithful step of obedience can you take?

4. Hope is defined as a "confident expectation." What can you confidently expect from God today?

5. How can you be a hope-filled person in your world? Can you name a specific idea for spreading hope this Christmas season?

* Advent Week *
— 2 —
ENCOUNTER PROVISION

"Love and large-hearted giving, when added together,
can leave deep marks. It is never easy to cover these
marks, dear friends— never easy."
-O. Henry, "The Gift of the Magi"

The love we feel at Christmastime is an invitation to
express ourselves through the act of giving.

But what do our beloved ones really desire from us?

Another thing to be added to a collection of things
collecting dust in forgotten corners?

*Perhaps Christmas is the time to develop a heart for
giving what others need, what we hope to receive in
return—those intangible sacrifices that cost us dearly
but are always worth it.*

*And when we fear we don't have "enough," when we
worry the cost is too high, we remember our Provider.*

*At Christmas, we remember that He gave everything
to give us what we really need.*

*At Christmas, we discover that He'll provide so we
can give others what they really need.*

Mark settled into his usual seat. The wooden pew, worn down through generations of use, told of the countless people who had used this same bench for prayer, meditation and reflection. He glanced up to find his son, Sam, squeezing in next to him.

So, Sam had decided to come. Mark wasn't sure he would after their argument the previous night. Maybe this was a good sign?

Looking down, Mark noticed the inches of space Sam had left between them—he was practically falling off the far edge of the pew.

Mark tried to catch his son's eye, to offer an appeasing smile. But Sam seemed absorbed by some detail on the other side of the room.

Maybe they weren't alright, after all.

Mark sighed. Well, if that's the way Sam wants it, Mark thought.

Soon enough, the service began. Father and son stood side by side, muttering the familiar choruses and Christmas carols along with the rest of the congregation.

To be honest, Mark wasn't focused completely on the service. Around the third verse of "Silent Night," his mind wandered back to their recent fight.

Nothing new was said, really. Mark just wanted the best for his son. Sam, an intelligent and vibrant 23-year-old, had yet to settle into a real career path. Since high school, he'd jumped from job to job, taking unpaid internships and even spending a semester "abroad" (Mark suspected that was a fancy word for "vacation").

He didn't want to deny Sam a full life of experiences. But when Mark had been Sam's age, he'd already completed a tour in the military and found a job working at the local auto body shop. In fact, he still worked at that shop; through hard labor and loyalty, he'd risen in the ranks to become assistant manager. Mark was proud of his work accomplishments and he wanted to share that same pride with his son. What was wrong with that?

But Sam didn't see it that way. In fact, they never saw anything the same way.

According to Sam, Mark was outdated. He didn't understand his son's creative ambitions or his sensitive worldviews.

Sam's accusations rang through Mark's memory.

"You don't support me." Sam's voice had been icy. "You never have."

"That's not true. I'm happy you have hobbies. I just worry you won't ever have a career."

"I'm working on that. Why do you think I'm in culinary school?"

Mark had shrugged, lost for words.

Sam continued, "Just so you know, I'm actually at the top of my class."

"And I'm proud of you for that, it's really neat. But it's not going to pay the bills." Why couldn't Sam see the sense of Mark's argument?

No, nothing new had been said. It was the same conversation they'd been having for years.

The night had ended with Sam storming out of the house, headed to God-knows-where. Mark hadn't seen him since then.

Now, Sam half-sang, half-hummed along with the music, artfully avoiding any contact with his dad.

Mark's attention was brought back to the service as the pastor climbed onto the stage. It was the season of Advent, preparing for Christmas. In the spirit of Christmas preparations, Mark began to think about his Christmas shopping list.

Then, he heard the pastor say:

"I want to challenge each of you. This Christmas, instead of buying something for someone, find an intangible gift you can give them. For many of us, it's easier to part with our money than it is to give something truly sacrificial, something that will cost us our time, our pride, our love."

Something began to burn in Mark. True, he could ignore this challenge and take the easy way out (it wouldn't be the first time). How simple would it be to buy Sam the latest trinket of technology?

Yet, this challenge sounded right—he felt it in his heart. He decided he would find an intangible gift to give Sam this year.

But what?

Sitting at a stoplight two days later, Mark considered his choice.

He'd just received a call from work—they wanted him back at the shop. They were swamped with last-minute repairs and could use an extra set of hands. Mark knew they could probably manage without him. But he also had inside information that the current general manager would be stepping down in the new year and the owners of the shop were eying replacements. Mark was the obvious choice to be the next general manager. He only needed to keep his head down and turn in the same solid work output as usual. And normally, Mark wouldn't hesitate to turn back to the shop, ready to clock in another late night. But tonight...

Well, tonight he had signed up for a class. After struggling to find an "intangible" gift that would show his son his support, Mark registered for a three-week culinary course through the local community center. Truthfully, he hadn't taken a class in decades and the fear of trying something new was almost enough to drive him back to the safety of his shop.

As he sat at the light trying to decide his next move, the words of the pastor echoed in his memory:

"...something that will cost us our time, our pride, our love."

The stoplight turned green, and Mark knew where he needed to go.

Two hours later, Mark stood from his workstation in the back of the community center. His fingertips were burned, his arm hairs singed, and his eyes watered from an onion encounter. And what did he have to show for all that? A burned pot roast.

For someone who worked with his hands every day, he was shocked to find how clumsy he was with the delicate maneuvers of slicing, peeling, whisking...not to mention all the skills he had yet to learn. The teacher had encouraged him throughout the night, but he suspected she was humoring him.

Stalking out to his car, his wounded pride began to rationalize the idea of quitting. After all, he thought, no one knew he'd signed up for the class. Who would care if he quit? He should accept that he wasn't a good cook and he never would be.

Not to mention that this silly class could cost him the promotion he'd been working toward. At something he was *actually* good at.

What was the point of all this, anyway? Sam still wasn't talking to him. Why did he think taking a class would make a difference?

Yes, he would quit. He would retreat back to work.

"...something that will cost us our time, our pride, our love."

There were those words again.

Well, he mused, this class was definitely costing time—time he could be putting in at the shop.

And, he had to admit, it was hurting his pride a bit. He wasn't used to looking like a fool.

He could think of all the things he was lacking, but he also knew he had something to give: his love.

Pausing in that darkened parking lot, he breathed a soft prayer. Though the challenge came from the pastor, Mark knew only God could grant him the patience and perseverance he would need to give this gift to his son.

"See you next week?" It was the teacher calling out as she walked to her car.

Mark raised his arm to wave, wincing from the pain in his wrist where he'd spilled hot oil. "See you then," he said.

Soft lights glowed from the Christmas tree. Peaceful music played in the background. But Mark didn't have time to notice any of it. He was too busy putting the final touches on his Christmas gift for Sam.

Three weeks of practice and patience, baking and burning, all led to this evening. As he peeked through the oven's glass, he had to admit that his pot roast finally looked right. It smelled pretty good, too.

When Mark had invited Sam to Christmas dinner, he could sense his son's hesitation. In the past, Christmas dinner had been lovingly prepared by Sam's mom. In the years since she'd been gone, it had fallen by the wayside. But after a brief pause, Sam had agreed to come over for dinner.

Mark came to a sudden stop in the center of his kitchen. What if Sam didn't like the dinner? If Sam was at the top of his class at culinary school, surely this would all seem silly to him. What did Mark really know about cooking anyway?

The experience of the past few weeks had shown Mark a few things. First of all, humbling oneself was an uncomfortable process. In fact, the line between humbling and humiliating was hard to determine at times. And second, he grew to respect and appreciate his son's hard work and dedication. Mark may not understand the artistic nature of Sam's choice of profession, but he couldn't deny that it required skill and perseverance. Maybe he had underestimated Sam.

As he set the roast on the table, surrounded by other small dishes he'd learned to cook at the community center, he heard a knock at the door.

Mark shifted nervously, unsure what to do next.

"Come in," he called.

Sam pushed open the front door, taking a moment to stomp the snow from his boots. He grew motionless as he took in the dining room scene.

Mark looked down to where he'd set the table with their family Christmas china and his simple dinner. He knew this must look paltry compared to past years, or even to Sam's new world of culinary experiences.

"Merry Christmas," Mark said, his voice cracking with emotion. "I, um, wanted to give you something different this year. Cooking's important to you. In fact, it's your career choice. I get that now. I know it's nothing fancy," he gestured to the table, "but...I did try hard." Unable to meet his son's eyes, Mark looked away.

Sam didn't move. He simply stared at the table.

After a moment, Mark coughed. "What do you think? You hungry?"

Finally, Mark looked into his son's eyes, surprised to find them filled with tears.

Without thinking, Mark crossed the room to his son, folding him into a hug. A hug that Sam returned. Tears turned to laughter as both father and son embraced.

"I can't believe you did this," Sam managed to say.

"It's all for you," Mark said with a smile. "So, should we eat?"

Sam took a step back. "Not yet. I have to give you my gift."

Mark raised his eyebrows in surprise. He hadn't once thought about what Sam was going to give him.

"You have to follow me outside." Sam grabbed Mark's hand and dragged him back through the front door, across the snow-covered front lawn and onto the street.

"Here you go, Dad," Sam said with a small flourish of the hand.

Mark looked to where Sam gestured and was confused to see...a car.

"This is my gift?" Mark was puzzled.

"Yes, well, in part." Sam's voice began to pick up speed with excitement. "See, remember when the pastor said we should do something for each other?"

Yes, Mark smiled, he remembered that.

"Well, I thought about what matters to you. And so, I bought this car. I know we weren't supposed to buy 'stuff.' But it's a clunker and on my evenings off, I've been learning how to restore it. You know, so I could understand the work you do. I'm afraid I didn't get very far, but I was hoping we could work on it together."

In his son's eyes, Mark saw the same vulnerability he'd been feeling only minutes ago. His whole being pulsed with warmth as he realized Sam had found his own way of expressing *"...something that will cost us our time, our pride, our love."*

"I would love that, Son."

And so, father and son shared a memorable Christmas evening, complete with laughter and love, a simple roast dinner and a ride around town in a half-rebuilt car. And these gifts were far more meaningful, because they were made up of the sacrificial and intangible qualities that make everything worthwhile.

In the bleak mid-winter
Frosty wind made moan;
Earth stood hard as iron,
Water like a stone;
Snow had fallen, snow on snow,
Snow on snow,
In the bleak mid-winter
Long ago.

What can I give Him,
Poor as I am?
If I were a Shepherd
I would bring a lamb;
If I were a Wise Man
I would do my part,
Yet what I can I give Him,
Give my heart.

"In the Bleak Midwinter"
Christina Rossetti

 Please take some time now to watch the video for this week's Advent focus. You can find the video at mattmessner.com/advent.

SCRIPTURE READING

Please have someone read aloud:

Matthew 2:3-6

King Herod was deeply disturbed when he heard this, as was everyone in Jerusalem. He called a meeting of the leading priests and teachers of religious law and asked, "Where is the Messiah supposed to be born?"

"In Bethlehem in Judea," they said, "for this is what the prophet wrote:

'And you, O Bethlehem in the land of Judah,
are not least among the ruling cities of Judah,
for a ruler will come from you
who will be the shepherd for my people Israel.'"

John 6:35

Jesus replied, "I am the bread of life. Whoever comes to me will never be hungry again. Whoever believes in me will never be thirsty."

CANDLE LIGHTING

While one person lights the candle, please have some one read:

This week, we light the second Advent candle. This is the Bethlehem Candle.
Bethlehem reminds us that God is our Provider.

In this place,
Mary gave birth
Shepherds worshiped
Angels sang
And a star lit the way.

There was no room at the inn, but God provided a manger.
Mary and Joseph didn't have much money, but God provided riches through the Magi.
A madman wanted to kill Jesus, but God provided a safe escape to Egypt.

Today, we know God provides for us. And as God provides for us, we give gifts to others.

PRAYER

Jesus,

We take this time to thank You for being our Provider.

You are the beginning of life, the source of abundance. Whatever we lack, we find in You.

May we give encouragement, as we often need it ourselves. Free our hearts from judgment.

May we give grace, as we all fall short of perfection. Remove all traces of condemnation.

May we give forgiveness, as we have been forgiven. Help us let go of all bitterness.

And may we give love, as we cannot live without it.

We do all these things in Your name and through Your provision,

Amen.

✶ DISCUSSION QUESTIONS ✶

1. What is your favorite part about giving during the Christmas season?

2. What is the most challenging part of giving?

3. What was the best gift you've ever given someone? (Remember, it doesn't have to be a physical object.)

4. What is something unseen or intangible that you can give someone this Christmas season?

5. How does God provide for you to give to others?

Advent Week
— 3 —
ENCOUNTER PURPOSE

There was once a very small girl who could see what others could not.

She appeared outside the grocer's market one snowy afternoon, and that was about all anyone could remember. She didn't stay very long, but she saw a great many people before she left.

The first person to remember seeing her was Mr. Dowdes, the grocer. She was a curious sight—all alone, sitting beside the homeless man who slept outside his shop. Through the window, he could see her talking, laughing and petting the man's cat.

Where is that child's mother or father? Dowdes glanced around the empty shop. No, her parents were not inside.

He nervously stepped outside and approached the pair huddled against the wall. The girl looked to be about eight years old, with curly brown hair pinned along the sides of her face. With wide eyes and an instant smile, she was the picture of innocence.

So what is she doing here? Talking with...him? Dowdes didn't know the homeless man's name. In fact, he barely noticed the man anymore.

"...I found her when she was a kitten," the homeless man was explaining to the child. "She's been my only family ever since."

The little girl nodded along with the man's story, like it made perfect sense to find a grown man swaddled in a sleeping bag outside a grocer's store with none for company but an ugly cat.

Dowdes shifted uncomfortably. He'd heard stories about homeless men before and his eyes scanned the street for a police officer or someone important (more important than him) to step in.

But the street was empty except for the three of them.

"Excuse me," Dowdes said to the little girl, turning so he spoke only to her.

"Alicia," she said.

"What a lovely name, Alicia. I'm Mr. Dowdes. Tell me, where are your parents?"

"My dad's just around the corner," Alicia said. "But he told me I could come meet the cat. And John."

"Is that the cat's name?"

Alicia began to giggle. "No, of course not. The cat is John's family."

Dowdes reddened as he realized his mistake. She was talking about the homeless man. He offered a brief smile to John, then turned his attention back to Alicia. John kept his eyes lowered.

"Well, it's a little cold out here, Alicia. Would you like to come inside and have some hot chocolate?"

Alicia's eyes grew bright with excitement. "I would love to!" She turned to the homeless man, "John, doesn't hot chocolate sound nice?"

Dowdes and John froze—they both knew that Dowdes' invitation had been for Alicia, and *only* her. But Alicia didn't seem to know this.

"I bet we can even bring Stinky inside with us." Alicia turned to Dowdes. "John can bring Stinky, right? Stinky is the cat, obviously."

After a pause, Dowdes managed a nod. "Sure, John can bring Stinky." What else could he say?

And so, the three—plus Stinky—headed inside for hot chocolate. They settled in the back room of the shop, where John served them warm mugs around a worn fireplace.

A silence descended on the group.

Dowdes took this time to observe John. In the light of the fire, Dowdes was surprised to see that John was much younger than he had assumed. No wrinkles, yet. Nor gray hairs. (The same things could not be said of Dowdes.) In fact, John looked to be about the same age as his own son, away at university.

Dowdes felt some of his fear replaced by curiosity. He knew where his son was; but who was concerned about John's whereabouts?

For the first time, Dowdes turned to address John.

"I heard you tell Alicia here that Stinky is your only family."

"Yes, sir." John stared into his mug.

"Well, how about your parents? Brothers, sisters? Anyone else?"

"Stinky's all I've got."

Dowdes shifted in his seat, unsure what to do with this information. "Did you move here, maybe from somewhere else?"

John shook his head. "I grew up here."

More puzzling information. Perhaps John had even gone to school with his son? And yet, Dowdes had never noticed him before.

"You grew up here and you've got no family? Who raised you then?"

"A few people over the years. You know," John shrugged one shoulder, "in the system."

"Did they send you to school?" Dowdes said, trying to keep the criticism out of his voice. "Make sure you were taken care of?"

"They tried their best."

Dowdes now felt utterly confused. "So then, how'd you end up..." The sentence trailed off into silence.

"Homeless?" John finished it for him. He paused, then replied, "I don't suppose it was one thing. To tell you the truth, no one's ever asked me that before. Well, except Alicia earlier today."

Alicia had been stroking Stinky's grimy hair while sipping her hot chocolate. But her eyes stayed focused on John, and, Dowdes could have been wrong here, but she seemed to listen with...a knowing compassion. *That's odd for a girl her age*, Dowdes thought.

Bolstered by her calm, Dowdes turned back to John. "If you'll tell me, John, I think I'd like to hear more of your story."

John glanced at Alicia, who nodded with a reassuring smile. Then he began to speak.

Together, they spent the next hour hearing the story of John's life.

The next sighting of Alicia involved the Parker twins—Bill and Mandy.

It was the twins' weekly visit to their mother, a resident of Autumn Pines Nursing Home. The visiting room was decorated for Christmas, with red and green tinsel hanging in doorways. As usual, they arrived at 3 p.m. on Tuesday afternoon. As usual, they ate dried cookies and showed her pictures of the grandkids. And as usual, they began eying their watches around 4 p.m., preparing excuses to leave.

In fact, everything about the visit was "usual." At first.

Throughout the hour, Bill and Mandy couldn't help but notice the little girl talking with the old man in the back corner of the visiting room. They recognized the old man as he often sat alone. No one ever came to see him.

But on this day, the tinkle of the child's laughter rippled through the room as the old man seemed to delight his young guest with stories. The effect was magnetic. Everyone—nurses, guests, visiting family members—turned their heads in the direction of the pair, curious to know the stories that inspired such joy.

At a different point in the hour, Bill and Mandy were surprised to see the little girl holding the man's hand, softly wiping away her tears. She placed her head on the old man's shoulder and the two sat in silence for a few minutes. Though the twins didn't know why, they felt the emotions of the little girl stir something within their own hearts.

When 4 p.m. rolled around, with the usual reasons for leaving, Mandy paused at the door. Bill, sensing her hesitation, nodded to her. Perhaps it was because they were twins, but he knew exactly what she was thinking. They both turned and walked toward the little girl and the old man in the back corner of the room.

"Excuse us, we don't want to interrupt," Mandy said.

"But we've never had the opportunity to meet your...grandfather, here," Bill said.

The little girl smiled and said, "Oh, this isn't my grandfather."

Great-grandfather? wondered Bill.

"This is my friend, Frank," she said. "And I'm Alicia."

"Nice to meet you both," Mandy said. "Do you mind if we join you?"

The twins settled into nearby chairs. Both were unsure why they felt compelled to meet Frank. They had never noticed him before, but today felt different.

Frank spoke up. "I was telling this young lady about my time in the war."

"Vietnam?" said Bill.

"World War II."

I'm 0-2. Maybe I should stop guessing things, thought Bill.

"And you still think about the war?" said Mandy.

"I think about it every day. It never leaves you, you know."

Neither Mandy nor Bill knew, but they nodded anyway.

"I was blown from a tank, you see. My friends, they died. And here I am at ninety-three years old, still living."

Mandy worried these stories were too graphic for Alicia, but the little girl didn't seem bothered. She just listened to Frank talk.

Frank told stories of joy, of sorrow, of loss, of life. And as he recounted adventures to his little audience in the back corner of the visitor's room, it became clear that these stories ran in circles through Frank's memory. He relived the past every day, over and over again.

"Do you know what they told me? They told me I have post-traumatic stress disorder from the war. But they didn't tell me that until 1995. I had PTSD for fifty years and didn't even know it! Imagine that."

But after hearing a few of Frank's stories, Bill and Mandy *could* imagine it.

"I don't want to keep you. I'm sure you've got important things to do," Frank said. "Hey, my own kids don't make it out here anymore. I guess my stories get old after a while."

Alicia grasped his hand and said, "Frank, you have so much wisdom to offer the world. You need to keep telling your stories, and we need to keep listening. I promise, others are going to learn so much from you."

At this, Frank sat up a little straighter.

What an odd thing for a girl her age to say, Bill thought.

Meanwhile, Mandy had an idea. "Frank," she said, "we come every week to see our mom. If it's alright with you, we'd also like to hear more of your stories."

"I think that would be alright," Frank said and Mandy couldn't be sure, but he appeared more dignified than when they'd arrived a few hours earlier.

When their visiting time was over, the Parker twins glanced back to see Alicia listening to Frank's next story.

Pastor Dave smiled in satisfaction. He'd just put the finishing touches on his Christmas sermon. Even he had to admit—he'd outdone himself this year. It would be a remarkable service.

But even with the sermon complete, there were still several more details to hammer out. A pastor's job is never done and there are certain

ADVENT WEEK 3 ENCOUNTER PURPOSE

times of the year when the work seems to multiply. Christmas is one of those times.

He walked among the pews, noting the windowsills needing dusting, the seat backs needing hymnals, the communion trays needing a polish. Still so much work to do, yet he was confident the service would be perfect. The thought filled him with gratification; after all, isn't that what the Lord deserved at Christmas? The perfect worship of the saints?

His thoughts were interrupted by a pounding on the front door.

Please don't be an emergency. He usually didn't mind the endless interruptions, but on this day, his schedule was filled with vital tasks and appointments.

Unlocking the door, he peeked outside to find the vexed faces of two young girls.

"Hi, Pastor Dave," the brown-haired girl said, "I'm Alicia, and this is my friend, Nancy."

Though he didn't recognize the girl, he assumed her parents were congregants—how else would she know his name?

"How can I help you, Alicia?"

"We need to use the restroom."

"Ah, I see." That explained their squirmy shuffling and wincing frowns.

"Come on in." Pastor Dave held open the door a little wider.

Both Alicia and Nancy darted to the restroom around the corner. Pastor Dave sighed with relief. This would be a short interruption, then he could resume his many tasks.

The girls returned a few minutes later, their appearance much more relaxed.

"Thanks for letting us in," Alicia said. "We were out playing and your church was the closest building with a restroom."

"Of course," Pastor Dave said. "Will your family be joining us for the Christmas service, Alicia?"

Alicia paused, then said, "I'll have to ask my dad. But my friend, Nancy, wants to come."

Pastor Dave turned to look at Nancy, realizing she hadn't said a word yet.

"Nancy and her parents would be most welcome."

Nancy remained expressionless.

"Oh, they've tried to come to a service here, but it doesn't work for them," Alicia said.

"I'm sorry to hear that." Pastor Dave was starting to wonder if he was missing something. "Anything I can do to help?"

"Let me ask Nancy." Alicia turned to her friend and began moving her hands in the air. After a few gestures, Nancy smiled and motioned her own hand signals.

Then it dawned on Pastor Dave: Nancy was deaf.

Alicia turned back to him. "Nancy says she would love to know what you're saying in the sermons. I imagine you spend a lot of time preparing all those words."

Pastor Dave thought back to the sermon he had finished that morning. He *was* quite proud of all the time he'd invested in creating a perfect message.

"All the songs, all the sermons, Nancy never knows what anyone's saying. That makes it hard to worship Jesus." Alicia paused in thought, then said, "Maybe, sometimes, we could worship a little differently, if it means everyone gets to worship."

And Pastor Dave began to wonder, what good was "perfect" if not everyone could take part? What was the value of his voice, if others were isolated in their silence? And how had he missed noticing Nancy all these years?

He looked at Alicia. *She has an odd amount of wisdom for a girl her age.*

Alicia smiled up at Pastor Dave. "Thanks again, Pastor. We'll see you around!"

With a few more hand motions to each other, Alicia and Nancy ran out the front door, eager to get on with their play.

As he relocked the front door, Pastor Dave thought back to his list of tasks and his tight schedule. He reflected on his carefully choreographed, perfect sermon and service. All Nancy wanted was to be included, to worship alongside everyone else.

Perhaps he could rethink a few things. It felt uncomfortable (what would people say if he changed the routine? would his service still be "perfect" if he stepped outside the lines?) but exciting, at the same time. Returning to his office, he felt a new sense of purpose in his walk.

Throughout the week, several more people met Alicia. Wherever someone was forgotten, overlooked or unseen, Alicia would sit down beside them. Whether incredibly visible, or utterly invisible, to Alicia, everyone had a purpose in the larger story of the community. She saw everyone.

And when Alicia left town, as suddenly as she appeared, each person could only guess at her real story. Was she a special child, gifted with the supernatural? After all, she *did* do and say many odd things. Was she an angel, sent to this commonplace community? Or a regular kid, filled with childlike wonder and curiosity in a world of busy, cynical adults?

No one would ever know the answer to these questions.

But if Alicia's behavior was some kind of magical, supernatural act, then she brought others into that magical place with her. For whom she saw, others began to see. Nothing escaped her notice, and others also began to notice, as well. Perhaps it was the kind of supernatural sight that everyone has access to.

There was once a very small girl who could see what others could not...until they did.

Truly He taught us to love one another
His law is love and His gospel is peace
Chains shall He break for the slave is our brother
And in His name, all oppression shall cease
Sweet hymns of joy in grateful chorus raise we
Let all within us praise His holy name

"O Holy Night"
Placide Cappeau
Trans. John Sullivan Dwight

 Please take some time now to watch the video for this week's Advent focus. You can find the video at mattmessner.com/advent.

Scripture Reading

Luke 2:8-20

That night there were shepherds staying in the fields nearby, guarding their flocks of sheep. Suddenly, an angel of the Lord appeared among them, and the radiance of the Lord's glory surrounded them. They were terrified, but the angel reassured them. "Don't be afraid!" he said. "I bring you good news that will bring great joy to all people. The Savior—yes, the Messiah, the Lord—has been born today in Bethlehem, the city of David! And you will recognize him by this sign: You will find a baby wrapped snugly in strips of cloth, lying in a manger."

Suddenly, the angel was joined by a vast host of others—the armies of heaven—praising God and saying, "Glory to God in highest heaven, and peace on earth to those with whom God is pleased."

When the angels had returned to heaven, the shepherds said to each other, "Let's go to Bethlehem! Let's see this thing that has happened, which the Lord has told us about."

They hurried to the village and found Mary and Joseph. And there was the baby, lying in the manger.

After seeing him, the shepherds told everyone what had happened and what the angel had said to them about this child. All who heard the shepherds' story were astonished, but Mary kept all these things in her heart and thought about them often. The shepherds went back to their flocks, glorifying and praising God for all they had heard and seen. It was just as the angel had told them.

CANDLE LIGHTING

While one person lights the candle, please have someone read:

The third Advent candle reminds us of the shepherds, the faithful watchers of the nearby flocks. They were regular people, just like you and me. The shepherds didn't always feel important or remembered.

But then, one magical night, the sky filled with angels. They sang of the birth of Jesus. A miracle was happening, and God wanted to include the shepherds!

Afterward, the shepherds shared their story with everyone who would listen.

We, too, are remembered and included.
We have Good News and joy to share.
We can worship Jesus, alongside the angels and shepherds.

No one is excluded; everyone is invited!

PRAYER

Jesus,

Your birth was a miracle. You bring the supernatural into our lives, and we are changed.

In our emotions, please take away our fear, anger and grief.
Instead, give us joy.

In our lives, show us our significance.
We are not invisible to You; help us see the "invisible" people in our world.

In our purpose, lead us to share the Good News with those who need it.
With You, we can bring joy into the lives of others.

In our passion, may we be vocal and not silent.
We want to tell Your story.

In Your name we pray,

Amen.

✳ DISCUSSION QUESTIONS ✳

1. Do you have a favorite story about miracles or magic? Why do you like it?

2. Have you experienced something miraculous in your life? (Remember, this could be big or small.)

3. Why do you think God chose shepherds to share the Good News?

4. In the video, we talk about a change in emotions, self-perception (how we see ourselves), purpose and passion. Which change do you need in your life?

5. What could be God's purpose for you this Christmas season?

Advent Week
— 4 —
ENCOUNTER BELIEF

The trail dust tasted grimy in my mouth. I winced in pain and slowly lifted my head off the ground.

What happened?

Replaying the last couple minutes in my mind, I could remember riding the trail, my mountain bike sailing over rocks and fallen branches. The wind was that perfect cool temperature of early December. Nothing slowed me down as I zipped along a path lined with old-growth fir trees.

So what had gone wrong? How did I end up on the ground, with a sore wrist and a backache?

I shook my head, trying to make sense of everything.

Yes, I had been riding along. Then, something had caught my eye.

A flash of gray.

A pair of yellow eyes.

A low growl.

A wolf.

Yes, that's what it was. I had spotted a gray wolf along the trail, so close I could have reached out and touched it.

A moment of tremendous fear had so distracted me that I had missed the divot in the path, which led to the crash, which led to my current state of injury and confusion.

My brain scrambled to sort out the details. Only about a hundred feet had passed between where I'd seen the wolf and where I'd fallen. So, the wolf could be nearby. In fact, at that moment, it could be running toward me...

I sat up straight, ignoring the pain in my back.

Where was the wolf?

Though I didn't know much about wolves, I was certain of this: they were wild, violent beasts. They're what the science community calls an "apex predator"—that means they are at the top of the food chain. No animal kills them; they do the killing.

I scanned the trail around me, looking for any sign of the wolf. Nothing.

I was safe.

I eased myself up off the ground, feeling for any broken bones. So far, only bruises and possibly a sprained wrist. To my greater surprise, my bike survived the fall better than I did. No popped tires or bent wheels. I'd be able to move on like nothing had happened.

This would make my wife, Bethany, happy. She wasn't thrilled I had taken the afternoon to go mountain biking. After our recent counseling session, I knew she wanted to get started on the homework assigned by the therapist. But I just needed...what was it I needed? Air? Space? Physical pain to distract me for a little while? Whatever it was I needed, I knew what she *didn't* need: a broken and injured husband to care for, right as her mom was coming to visit for the holidays.

Releasing a sigh of relief, I mounted my bike, anxious to get back on the path. Still, a thought was nagging me, and I couldn't quite push off the ground. It was about that wolf.

Gray wolves had been extinct in this forest for almost a century. In fact, I couldn't recall the last time a wolf was heard of in this part of the state.

And yet, I had seen one.

I felt torn. Should I leave, forgetting what I saw? Or did I have a greater responsibility—to science, to the public, to myself—to document what I saw? Not to mention, a little adventure would provide more distraction from the impending couple's counseling homework.

Pulling my cell phone from my waterproof jacket, I dismounted from my bike and tucked it against a nearby tree.

I had a new mission: to find and photograph the extinct gray wolf.

I should mention that I knew this wasn't the best plan, but I couldn't stop myself. Armed with nothing but a bicycle helmet and a cell phone without service, I inched back to where I had last seen the wolf, some one hundred yards up the trail.

I tried to remember what I'd learned through TV nature shows. For bears, a person should yell and make loud sounds. For hyenas, a person should contort themselves to appear bigger. And for wolves, a person should never, ever run away.

What would the TV nature shows say about trying to photograph one? They probably wouldn't recommend it.

And yet, there I was, hunched over, creeping in the direction of a wild predator. I couldn't say why I did it; maybe I just needed to know that what I saw was real. That happens to me sometimes—I *believe* something, but then I need a little more proof.

I saw a gray wolf, that much I believed. But a photo would go a long way in proving it.

I rounded the last bend in the trail, almost at the spot I remembered.

Kneeling behind a giant fern, I peeked my head from behind a leaf, worried I would find myself face-to-face with those terrible yellow eyes.

And there, where the wolf had crouched only moments before, I saw...

Nothing.

The path was empty.

I don't know why I expected the wolf to be there, and yet, I felt disappointment. Now how would I know that what I believed was actually real?

The thing about couple's counseling is that you have to believe in it for it to work. If you don't believe in it, then there's no point in trying to track down a solution.

Bethany said that God wants healing for us. She believes He's real—no, more than that, she *knows* God is real.

For me, belief was good. Proof would have been better. Something I could see, something I could touch. If I *knew* God was real, then I would know that healing was possible for our marriage. But without proof, was it all in my mind? Just wishful thinking?

The wolf was gone.

But maybe it didn't go far.

Picking myself up, I felt more determined than ever to find and photograph the animal. I held up my phone camera in front of my face, confident that at any moment, the beast would appear in front of me.

True, the patch of dirt where the wolf had stood was now empty, but it wasn't without markings. I knelt down in the mud and took pictures of the prints—definitely canine, though larger than a regular dog's impressions.

It wasn't a wolf itself, but it was a sign of a wolf. It had been there. I didn't imagine it.

Smiling, I could now get back on the trail. I had my proof.

But was it enough? a thought whispered. Who would believe a phone photo of a paw print? After all, many claimed to have footprint casts of Bigfoot, and that wasn't enough to believe in *his* existence.

Some could even argue it was just a coyote. They could be right.

In the end, my doubts convinced me that I needed to see the wolf again. With my own two eyes. It was the only way to know it was real.

Thinking of Bethany, I was sure she wouldn't approve of this plan. *I* didn't even approve of this plan. But I was committed.

I tapped the flashlight symbol on my phone and took several cautious steps into the forest shadows. With every few yards, I leaned a branch against a tree to mark my path.

I didn't go far before I stumbled upon my next sign: the leftovers of a recently devoured meal. I won't go into the details of it here, but trust me, it wasn't a pretty sight. Entrails on trails, I thought. The poor animal never saw the predator coming.

And yet, I was pursuing that same wolf. What did that say about me?

I snapped a few photos; this was more proof. Now, in addition to my initial sighting, I had two signs of the wolf's existence.

It's not that I didn't believe in God or in healing. There had been signs in the past.

A little while ago, Bethany and I had gone through a medical scare. And a few years before that, we were in some desperate financial troubles. In all those circumstances, everything generally worked out. Not always the way we wanted, or in the timing we wanted. But it did work out.

So why did I have doubts now? I had the signs, I know what I saw happen in the past.

How many signs did I need to confirm that what I believe is real? How much proof would be enough?

I continued on through the forest. Out there, away from the people and the traffic, one could find absolute silence. Absolute peace.

Suddenly, the silence was cut, ripped open by a long, mournful howl.

The sound came from nearby. The wolf was close. Perhaps it stood just a few feet ahead of me, concealed in the thick underbrush. I raised my camera.

After all the signs, and the pursuit. After having only my belief, I would finally get undeniable evidence.

I waited for movement, aware that the next few moments would be dangerously unpredictable. But it would be worth it, right?

I held my breath.

Then, I heard branches snap under the weight of an approaching animal.

The sounds moved closer to me.

The tree to my left began to shake.

This was it.

I turned to the left, ready for whatever I would encounter.

But I wasn't ready for what stepped out of those woods.

"Are you lost?" asked the park ranger, dressed in a pressed green uniform.

I stood there in shock, unmoving. Then, I swung my head around, trying to see everywhere at once.

Where was the wolf? It was right here!

I had prepared myself to finally confirm what I thought I had seen: an extinct wolf. Instead, all I saw was a middle-aged ranger with a very manly beard.

"Excuse me, sir. Are you lost?" The park ranger's voice sounded concerned. To be fair, I'm sure I seemed a little odd.

I cleared my throat. "Ah, no. Thank you. My mountain bike is over there." I pointed in the direction of the trail.

"That's good to hear. You know, you shouldn't be out here. It's not safe to wander off the trail."

I nodded. He was right, after all. "I'm heading out now. It's just that I thought I saw..."

"Yes?"

"Have you ever heard of wolves living out here?"

The ranger's eyebrows shot up. "Wild wolves? Nope, no wolves. They haven't been in these parts for almost a hundred years."

I deflated as all the energy left my body. The ranger said no wolves, and he was the expert.

"OK," I said, trying to hide my disappointment. "I thought I saw one, but I can't be sure."

"Well, thanks for telling me. I'll keep an eye out in case anyone else reports a wolf sighting. You never know," he said with a shrug.

Whether he was humoring me, or he believed it possible, I would never know.

With a small wave, I turned back to the trail. I found my bike where I had left it and continued my descent down the mountain.

When I arrived home that evening, I was covered in mud and sweat. Not exactly the picture of cleanliness for Bethany, but she didn't complain about it. I always appreciated that about her.

We sat down for dinner and I told her about the gray wolf and my adventure while tracking it. She listened with wide eyes, forgetting all about her food.

As I expected, she wasn't thrilled to hear about some of my decisions, but I was surprised to find she believed me. Every single word.

"Here," I pulled out my phone, "these are some of the photos I took. See? These are the paw prints. And this—this is clearly what the wolf ate earlier today." (In hindsight, dinner probably wasn't the best time to show her photos of a leftover animal carcass.)

"That's an incredible story," she said, handing the phone back to me.

I hesitated, then said, "But you believe me, right?"

"Of course I do," she said. "Even without these photos, I would have believed you."

"So you don't think it was wishful thinking? Or my imagination playing tricks on me? I don't need more proof?"

"Belief isn't about getting a photo or some other proof. It's about choosing to believe what you know in your heart."

I smiled, relief filling my body. Perhaps, even without the proof I had been chasing, I could believe, I could *know*, that what I saw was real.

"Hey, Bethany," I said, nodding toward our marriage counseling book on the end table. "After dinner, would you like to work on some of our homework together?"

All praise to Thee, Eternal Lord,
Who wore the garb of flesh and blood;
And chose a manger for Thy throne,
While worlds on worlds were Thine alone.

Once did the skies before Thee bow;
A virgin's arms contain Thee now;
While angels who in Thee rejoice
Now listen for Thine infant voice.

"All Praise to Thee, Eternal Lord"
Martin Luther

 Please take some time now to watch the video for this week's Advent focus. You can find the video at mattmessner.com/advent.

SCRIPTURE READING

Please have someone read aloud:

Matthew 1:20-24

But after he had considered this, an angel of the Lord appeared to him in a dream and said, "Joseph son of David, do not be afraid to take Mary home as your wife, because what is conceived in her is from the Holy Spirit. She will give birth to a son, and you are to give him the name Jesus, because he will save his people from their sins."

All this took place to fulfill what the Lord had said through the prophet: "The virgin will conceive and give birth to a son, and they will call him Immanuel" (which means "God with us").

When Joseph woke up, he did what the angel of the Lord had commanded him and took Mary home as his wife.

Candle Lighting

While one person lights the candle, please have someone read:

Today, we light the fourth candle of Advent. This is the Angel Candle.
Messengers from God, the angels carry important messages to people throughout the Christmas story.

The angel told Mary and Joseph of a baby to be born, called "Immanuel," which means "God with us."
A multitude of angels proclaimed Jesus' birth to the shepherds who were watching their sheep by night.
And in the future, an angel will herald the return of Jesus.

We, too, can carry important messages to the people around us. When we believe the Christmas story, we can joyfully share it with everyone.

God is with us, and we are with each other.

PRAYER

Jesus,

Thank You for being "God with us." Because of Your birth, we no longer have to be alone.

May we follow Your example and learn to share our lives with each other as You share Your life with us.

We accept the joy that comes with the Christmas celebration. We step out in faith. Though we don't have all the answers today, we know one day, all the answers will be found in You.

This Christmas, we declare that
We believe You are God, and that You took on human form.
We believe You lived, died and rose again to give us life.
We believe You love us.
We believe.

Amen.

✳ DISCUSSION QUESTIONS ✳

1. How is believing in Jesus different than some of the other things people might believe about Christmas?

2. Immanuel means "God with us." How do you feel that God is with you throughout the day?

3. Jesus shared His life with us. If we follow Jesus' example, then we should share our lives with others. What is one way you could share your life with someone tomorrow?

4. In the past, have you ever expected something great to happen, and then it did? Share about that experience.

5. What is one thing you are believing for or expecting from God in the near future?

* Advent Week *
— 5 —
ENCOUNTER CHRISTMAS

For some, Christmas was an event. A one-night interruption in their daily lives.

For others, Christmas was a journey. A once-in-a-lifetime quest to find answers.

These others were the Magi.

Little is known about their number, origin or identity. But we know they traveled far, guided by the light of a star.

Two months on the road

I look into the heavens and I see it again—the star. I know I should grow tired of seeing it there, hanging above us, but every time, it delights me anew. What an exciting time to be alive!

In the evenings, I step from my tent and gaze skyward, afraid we will find it gone. One day it appeared; is it so hard to believe that one day it will disappear again?

I pray we find the great King before that happens.

On this journey, I share my tent with my husband. It's too big for the two of us, but soon we will be joined by a third. If our dates are correct, and we pride ourselves on our accurate timekeeping, then in just a few months' time, a baby will be ours to love and raise. We have been married for six years and still no child of our own. But this will change soon!

A new star. A new journey. A new King. And a new baby. Yes, an exciting time!

Tonight, there is great joy throughout the camp. We have made quick progress, passing through the deserts and along the dried river beds. Our camels are strong and carrying us with purpose. Maybe they, too, know how important this King is?

We eat our dinner, tell stories and chart the movement of the stars by the light of our campfire. Someone, somewhere, is singing a happy song.

About seventy left Persia behind to go on this journey. We are leading this expedition, and we are the Magi. Priests and astronomers who follow the teachings of Zoroaster, we study the ways of the world, devoting ourselves to truth and discovery. We can say, without pride, that we are the leading scholars of the sky, the healers, the wise.

Of course, not all in our group are Magi. With us, we bring cooks, attendants, guards and animal herders. This is a long pilgrimage and we are prepared.

As for my place in everything, I did not choose to be a Magi. It is a social class within our community. I was born into it, as was my husband, as will my child. And as a family, we hope to discover something new: the infant King for whom the star glows.

Some Magi believe the King will bring a great war. This world is covered with wars—perhaps this is what all kings desire?

Others say he will be rich beyond imagination. I have never met a king who did not possess a great fortune, so this does seem possible.

But there have been stirrings in our own teachings, whispered prophecies of a savior. Personally, this is what I hope we find, for this is what we need most.

And so, we watch the star in the sky, praying it will stay lit long enough for us to complete our journey.

Seven months on the road

I am heartbroken.

My baby is gone. It happened suddenly and then it was over.

What good is all our study and science if it cannot save the life of my child? We Magi are known throughout the region as the most knowledgeable, with every resource available to us. And yet, all my years of learning cannot comfort me now. How hollow everything seems—where is the hope?

There it is, again. That star. What does it know of my grief and disappointment?

I want to give up and turn home. This road is much longer and harder than I imagined.

My husband, he, too, grieves. We had so many hopes of starting a family. But this is the third child we've lost in as many years, and I do not know if we can continue like this.

In the past, I would pull out my charts and instruments, devoting hours to marking and measuring the path of the star. But tonight, I just lie under its light. With my finger, I trace its path, leading me forward. It doesn't stop for me, so I must decide if I will continue.

As if it can hear my thoughts, the star blinks in the sky.

Don't go away, I beg. I've lost too much.

And then I know, I must go on.

I am unsure what we'll find at the end of this road, but the light is stronger than the dark. It blinks, but it remains.

The next morning, we pack up camp. My husband barely says a word. I know he hurts as I do. But as we fold our blankets and load our donkeys, he stands next to me and our hands touch. I look to him, and he offers me a small smile. We will continue together.

Our caravan is anxious to make better time. The weather is growing hotter and there is less water to be found in this stretch of desert. To make matters worse, these hills with their hidden caves are known for holding bandits and thieves. It seems danger and death are hunting us down. Will we die of thirst? Or of attack? We don't speak these questions aloud, but we all think them.

Above all, there is one question burning in each of our hearts:

Is this King worth the journey?

Are we willing to give our lives to meet this baby?

Twelve months on the road

The star has stopped.

And so have we.

In fact, none of us can move; we are frozen in suspense.

Have we really found the new King? Is our journey finally at its end?

In all our travels, the star never faded nor disappeared. Even now, it blazes in the sky above us…and above the humble house before us.

We are in the land of the Jews, near the city of Jerusalem. I had expected to find the new King in such a city. It seemed the perfect home for a King of the Jews. (In fact, there was already a king there, named Herod.)

But the star prompted us onward, to this small town filled with shepherds and shopkeepers.

I will admit, of all the things I imagined over the past year, all the things I hoped for—I never anticipated something so…ordinary.

The house looks like my old grandmother's house. A simple structure, made of earth. Nearby, I hear a carpenter hammering in his shop.

These are normal people with normal lives.

But this is where the light has led us. I dismount my camel.

It has been decided that I will be the first to enter the house. For us, a woman should not be alone with a man who isn't her husband, and so I will greet the mother of the King.

As I approach the house, I listen for crying or whimpering, the sounds of a baby. But I hear nothing.

What if they aren't home? What if we missed them?

I knock on the door and call out.

The door opens, and I am greeted by a girl—possibly the age of my youngest sister. She's sixteen this year.

"Are you the mother of the King?"

With curiosity, she looks over my shoulder to see our entourage, each member holding their breath, awaiting her answer.

She smiles and nods.

From behind me, I hear the cries of joy break out. I can't help it, I begin to laugh.

This is it!

"May we come in and meet him?"

Again, she nods and moves aside.

Stepping into the shaded house, my eyes take a moment to adjust. In the absence of sight, I hear a baby cooing in the corner. I can sense his sweet smell—all the babies ever born have that same fragrance, and yet, there's nothing else like it in the entire world.

Then, I can see him. The new King. The one so worthy of worship that the Heavens themselves led us here.

And in him, I see a baby. Not unlike the baby I had hoped to have by now.

My arms ache to pick him up, and I turn to the mother.

"What is your name?" I ask her.

"Mary."

"Mary, may I hold him?"

"Of course."

And so, I do. As I gently raise him from his bed, he looks at me. And though it's hard to explain, I do believe he *understands* me. As a tear slips down my cheek, his chubby hand reaches out and touches my face. When he smiles, I sigh in peace. I am complete.

After an eternity compressed into a mere moment, I return the child to his bed. There is other work to do here.

I return to the caravan outside and instruct the waiting Magi to bring our gifts. Looking back at the house, I am happy we chose to bring gold, frankincense and myrrh. It looks like they could use it.

The Magi file inside; the space can hardly contain us all, for we are many and the home is small. I watch as each greets young Mary and then approaches the bed holding the infant King.

My husband is the first to fall to his knees. But soon, the rest of us follow.

Here is the source of the light. We found the one for whom we searched.

It is an emotional day. While the others linger in the house, I step outside for a breath of fresh air.

As I sit beneath the shade of a tree, Mary sits beside me.

She is quiet for many minutes, as am I.

Then I say, "You are a very lucky woman."

"I am blessed," she replies.

I nod. If she is blessed, then what am I? Cursed?

"And you?" she says, sensing my pain. "Are you blessed?"

"Not with children. Not like you."

"But He isn't really mine, you know. He belongs to His Father and to the world."

"Even still, you have a baby to hold."

"And I worry for the day when I can hold Him no longer."

"Why do you say these things? Won't your son be a powerful King? We came all this way because we believe he is someone special."

Mary's eyes grow wide. "Oh, He's special," she pauses, "but maybe not in the way you imagine."

"Then tell me."

She thinks for a moment, then says, "He is the Messiah—that is what the angels told us, me, my husband, the shepherds." Mary grows serious, much too serious for a girl her age. "But the prophets tell us that the savior will live a hard life."

A hard life. After this past year, I know that feeling.

"He will have to give up everything. But through Him, we will have healing. Through Him, we will have life. And through Him, we will have light in the darkness."

Healing. Life. Light.

For these, I would gladly travel the world. For these, I would sacrifice and suffer. For these are the deepest desires of my heart. The star, a light in the sky, led us here, to the light of the world.

I look up as my husband approaches. He wears a hint of a smile. "We will return home soon," he says. "Are you ready?"

"I'm ready," I reply. "Ready for whatever's next."

And so, we look to the light and follow its call. It is not a single event, but an ongoing journey into the unknown.

Healing. Life. Light.

Christmas.

What star is this, with beams so bright,
A stranger midst the orbs of light?
It shines to herald forth the King,
Glad tidings of our God to bring.

While outward signs the star displays,
An inward light the Lord conveys,
And urges them with force benign,
To seek the Giver of the sign.

Oh, while the Star of heavenly grace
Invites us, Lord, to seek Thy face,
May we no more that grace repel,
Or quench the light which shines so well.

"What Star Is This, with Beams So Bright"
Charles Coffin
Trans. John Chandler

 Please take some time now to watch the video for this week's Advent focus. You can find the video at mattmessner.com/advent.

SCRIPTURE READING

Please have someone read aloud:

Isaiah 9:2; 6-7

The people who walk in darkness
will see a great light.
For those who live in a land of deep darkness,
a light will shine.

For a child is born to us,
a son is given to us.
The government will rest on his shoulders.
And he will be called:
Wonderful Counselor, Mighty God,
Everlasting Father, Prince of Peace.
His government and its peace
will never end.
He will rule with fairness and justice from the throne
of his ancestor David
for all eternity.
The passionate commitment of the Lord of Heaven's
Armies will make this happen!

CANDLE LIGHTING

While one person lights the candle, please have someone read:

Today, we light the final candle of Advent. This is the Jesus Candle, a reminder that He is the brightest light in our world.

The entire Christmas story revolves around the baby Jesus—we celebrate today *because of* Him and *for* Him.

Though He was a baby, He was already our Savior, our Messiah. He was born into darkness to be the light of the world. We see His light in our lives, and we each have the choice to follow Him.

PRAYER

Jesus,

Thank You for Your birth.
Thank You for Your life.
Thank You for Your death.
And thank You for Your resurrection.

We know You are alive today. We celebrate that you are our healing, our light, our life.

You are greater than any darkness; let Your light fill our lives today.

If we are lost, show us the way.
If we need hope, lead us forward.
If we need direction, illuminate the path.

We look to You; we wait on You.

You are all we need.

We love You and follow You,

Amen

✳ DISCUSSION QUESTIONS ✳

1. Has there ever been a time you were lost in the dark? How did you find your way out?

2. The Magi left everything behind to follow the Bethlehem star. What do you think was the hardest part of following the star?

3. Has God ever led you to do something that scared you? What was that like?

4. Where do you see God's light in your life?

5. After all the weeks of Advent preparation we've done, what does Christmas personally mean to you today?

Acknowledgments

Many thanks to:

Pastors Jim and Betsey Hayford: They introduced us to family Advent readings over 25 years ago and provided us with the inspiration for this book.

Rachel McMurray-Branscombe: Without her encouragement, initiative and investment, this book would not have been written. Thank you for coming alongside us to make this possible.

Eric Wilson: For his ongoing insight, feedback and encouragement, we are especially grateful. His creativity and God-given skills as a writer continue to inspire us.

Leslie and Scott Lemmon, Amy McKnight, Harvey Family, Sherman Family: Each gave their time freely to contribute their unique perspective to this book. Thank you for being our readers.

How to Contact the Author

You can email Matt Messner directly at matt.messner@gmail.com.

Notes

How to Use This Book

Filz, Gretchen. "The Advent Wreath Tradition and Meaning." Get Fed. November 14, 2016. Accessed September 24, 2018. https://www.catholiccompany.com/getfed/the-advent-wreath-tradition-meaning/.

Holcomb, Justin. "What Is Advent?" Christianity.com. Accessed September 24, 2018. https://www.christianity.com/christian-life/christmas/what-is-advent.html.

Reeves, Ryan. "The History of Advent." The Gospel Coalition (TGC). November 28, 2016. Accessed September 24, 2018. https://www.

thegospelcoalition.org/blogs/ryan-reeves/the-history-of-advent/.

Advent: Encounter Christmas

Ashby, Chad. "Magi, Wise Men, or Kings? It's Complicated." Christianity Today. December 16, 2016. Accessed September 24, 2018. https://www.christianitytoday.com/history/2016/december/magi-wise-men-or-kings-its-complicated.html.

Drum, Walter. "Magi." *The Catholic Encyclopedia*. Vol. 9. New York: Robert Appleton Company, 1910. Accessed September 24, 2018. http://www.newadvent.org/cathen/09527a.htm.

Ebrahimpour, Tamara. "Women's Rights in Ancient Persia." Iran Review. May 18, 2008. Accessed September 24, 2018. http://www.iranreview.org/content/Documents/Women_s_Rights_in_Ancient_Persia.htm.

Schenk, Christine. "An Epiphany with Wise Women?" National Catholic Reporter. January 07, 2016. Accessed September 24, 2018. https://www.ncronline.org/blogs/simply-spirit/epiphany-wise-women.

CPSIA information can be obtained
at www.ICGtesting.com
Printed in the USA
JSHW010658021219
2727JS00001B/2